LISTENING TO THE CORN

THE HEARTBEATS OF LIFE ALL AROUND

BY

RITA BRESNAHAN

'Listening to the Corn' Copyright © 2013 by Rita Bresnahan
All rights reserved. Published in the United States by Rita Bresnahan.

All rights reserved. The use of any part of this publication transmitted in any form or by any means, electronic, mechanical, photocopying, recording, or otherwise, or stored in a retrieval system, without the prior consent of the author is an infringement of the copyright law.

Book and Cover Design: Vladimir Verano, Third Place Press

Cover photography : © Gordo25 via istockphoto.com

Author photo © Rita Bresnahan

Author contact: *namaste7@comcast.net*

ISBN: 978-0-9899881-0-0

Printed at Third Place Press, Lake Forest Park, WA
on the Espresso Book Machine v.2.2.
www.thirdplacepress.com

This book is dedicated to You.
You, holding this book.

You, the people I/we meet every day in common ordinary places.
You who make poems of your lives, even when you may not know it.
You who delight, inspire, surprise, chagrin, dismay, listen…
who cause something to shift inside when our lives overlap, even briefly.
You who make others wonder and question, make us catch our breath, reminding
us to appreciate life in all its wondrous faces…

Yes, you…holding this book.
I dedicate it to you.

CONTENTS

GRATITUDES — *i*

PREFACE — *iii*

LISTEN TO THE CORN — *v*

Keep Smiling — 1

Moosley-um-plee-puss
Hoo-eeeet, hoo-eeeeeee-oo
Tykes Take Mommy "Out" for Dinner
"Keep Smilin'"
Spoiled

From the Mouths of Babes — 15

Remember How to Do Cartwheels
Kindness in Disneyland
The Microphone Tree
Lavender Brushing
"Are You Happy?"
Namaste

Prejudices — 31

Spikes
The Bhagavad Gita in Iraq
Northern Lights

Silly Silly   39

A Holey Time
Imposter Aunt
Surprise Surprise
Rats!
Quirky
Weighing In
Failing my Physical

We Are Crone   57

Yellow Blanket Babies
Turd into Trillium
A Breath Away
Just Build Fires Together
Good Medicine

Beginnings and Endings   77

Love Cycles
Born Again Boots
Our Tears Run Together
Boat Whisperers
Footprints
Jubilee Reflection

Gratitudes

First I wish to thank all the people I've encountered in these stories, especially those of you in my dear family. And to the many others I've met by chance—when our lives happened to cross paths for only a few brief moments…

Also I am deeply grateful to:

…my sister, Mary Smoluch, for her superb editing and enduring support.

…my neighbor Shelly Fields, who first dubbed me "writer Rita" and continues to encourage me to get my stories "out there."

…my many friends, who have listened and listened to my stories over the years, and graciously shared theirs with me.

…Peggy Sturdivant, friend and writer par excellence, who serves as writing midwife each week for so many

…my spirited and spunky writing/reading/listening buddies over many years at Cancer Lifeline, in whose presence many of these stories caught their first breath.

…the Ballard Writers Collective, especially Peggy, Jeanette, Claire, Roselle, and Ingrid for their encouragement, guidance, and hands-on assistance.

…Vladimir Verano, who meticulously and masterfully transformed my manuscript into a real live book: *Listening to the Corn*.

Thank you and bless you all.

PREFACE

I'm dubbing this book my "jubilee opus."

I turn 80 years old just as "Listening To the Corn" is being launched.

This "opus" has been a long time in the making…

As the past year began drawing to a close, I said to myself (and friends had echoed similar sentiments), "Rita, you have tons of stories, and some go way back, even years. You keep promising to do something with them…" That's true. Should I?

So I began dialoguing with my stories: "I think this is your last chance. It's now or never." They sassed me back: "Don't keep stringing us along, like you're going to use us. You're just teasing us!" Hmmm. "Okay, I'll do something," I promised.

Well, I'm keeping my word. Here it is: a small collection of slices of life that I capture—and that capture me. Simple human interest stories. Some about family, others about children, assumptions I find myself making about people, silly encounters, stories of beginnings and endings. So many lessons learned. The thread of listening weaves itself throughout—whether with children or my age-mates, and in such diverse places as a grocery store, a conference room, a nursery, an airport. Sometimes my funny bone gets tweaked in most unexpected ways.

As reflected in the lead story, for me, "listening to the corn" means listening deeply to one another, even to what is unspoken, to what "corn" might represent for each person. The core: where a person is most alive, what really matters to him or her. Listening in this way, we are able to immerse ourselves in one another's words and experience.

Listening to the corn also means listening to oneself, to messages from one's body, and one's intuition. It means paying attention to the heartbeat of life as it happens all around us. Nudging and poking and uplifting, astonishing and swirling, questioning, and blessing...

I've often fancied myself to be an aspiring poet, but captivating stories keep happening that elbow latent poems right out of my moving pen. That's a "listening" all its own, and in a way, is how I greet life each day--alert for "poems" all around. What I mean here by "poems" are really poetic moments that present themselves in living color before my very eyes. I love catching stories as they happen. Often they come tumbling through my days so quickly... I can scarcely keep up with them or remember to record the most compelling ones.

Fellow writers and other friends have asked how I remain aware, how I hone the treasure of discovering simple poems in everyday kinds of happenings. Well, I really work at it, make it a daily practice. Often I set an intention to watch for, listen for, a "poem," for example, in the next hour. Or at such and such event. Or on the bus today. On my walk today. Or with the children. Given this focus, each of my senses becomes highly attuned to what is going on in that particular environment, and I gain an even deeper appreciation for my surroundings. Never am I disappointed, never at a loss. The "poems" that pop up often feel like holy moments.

The remarkable Storycorps Project declares that "...listening is an act of love"--based on the premise that "if we take the time to listen, we'll find wisdom, wonder, and poetry in the lives and stories of the people all around us."

Listening to the Corn seconds the motion, bearing witness to that truth.

LISTEN TO THE CORN

My brother Bob is dying. It is the last summer he will see.

Bob knows it. We all know it. Leukemia. It's been in remission and now is back running in his blood again. This time, all possibilities are exhausted. No longer can he hope to see his three daughters graduate from high school, although for the oldest, that is less than a year away. Father of six children, he is bargaining for that: "I'm only 49. I want to see my girls raised, at least out of high school."

Realizing he will not get his wish, he shakes his fist at each visitor who stops by, and shouts bitter words, "Where is your God of mercy?"

No one has an answer.

All his life Bob has been a farmer. From the time he was a little boy, he spent his days outdoors, often building an imaginary farm in the dirt behind the house, or constructing elaborate farms out of cardboard boxes. He loved farm animals and farm implements, and would play with those toys in his "farms" for hours. He'd talk to them, and even listen to them. Each Christmas, he would lift the cows, the sheep, and the donkey out from the Bethlehem crib under the tree and haul them around for a ride in his toy dump truck or on his little green tractor. Day-dreaming, he'd often sit on his haunches staring into space, as if he were hearing something, listening to the soundtrack of a distant dream.

Though he never actually lived on a farm, Bob hoped to, and bought acres and acres of fertile farmland in Illinois and in Iowa. "This is God's Country," he frequently reminded those of us who had left.

He began creating a company of his own, buying a dump truck one year and a farm implement another – real ones this time – until after some years he owned a fleet of trucks himself. "Bob K. Bresnahan" he proudly emblazoned on the door of each cab. Late summer evenings he relished walking the cornfields he had treated earlier that day with fertilizer from Farm Supply. Both arms outstretched, brushing the stalks on either side of him as he examined the fruits of his labor. I could imagine him stopping in the middle of one row, looking, listening. Pausing countless rows further, listening again, deeply–ear cocked to the soil–or up to the spacious sky–or into the heart of the grain. He became one with the land.

This "last Bob-summer," as I make my annual summer trek back to roots country, I have a favor to ask of Bob. In the Northwest, I have embarked on the study of Native American tradition, and I've promised to bring some Illinois corn back to use in a ceremonial circle ritual. I tell Bob what I'm wanting, and ask, "Could we go out to your fields sometime to pick a few ears of corn?" He seems surprised, even pleased.

There's a catch in his voice as he responds, "Sure…when shall we go?" We make plans to meet the next day. "You'll have to drive, though," he reminds me, apologetically.

Even though Bob is four years younger than I, never have I driven him. He would not have allowed it. So I'm slightly anxious when I pick him up. It's a scorching hot August afternoon in Illinois—temperature over 100 degrees, humidity at its peak. Heat waves emanate from the blacktop. We crank up the air-conditioning.

"My fields are just outside town," he informs me. After less than a mile, he directs, "Turn left at the next lane." Seeing no opening, I nearly pass it. "There!" he points, "in there!" Obediently, I turn onto a lane so narrow it can scarcely accommodate a vehicle. I nose the car gingerly in under laden cornstalks.

"Park here," he orders.

We get out of the car, the relentless mid-afternoon sun beating down on us. Suddenly I realize that in all these years I have been returning to roots country, never have I set foot on his beloved fields. I have not even laid eyes on them, ever entered into the joy of his work. I have not known the core of this man, my brother. Overcome with emotion, I stand—mute, motionless, regretful—in his field.

Bob steps slowly onto his land, onto the soil he has tilled, planted, and harvested for nearly thirty years. Hunched, and quite weak, he begins walking, squinting up at the majestic swaying stalks, first along one row, then another. I follow close behind, not sure what he is looking at or listening for. Finally, he reaches up, draws one of the stalks down to eye-level, pulls back a husk, turns and asks, "What about this one, Reet?"

"Oh that's a perfect one, Bob!"

We repeat this ritual several times, until I say, "We have enough now."

He, too, seems satisfied—or perhaps, simply spent. As we return to the car bearing our armload of corn, he leans heavily on my shoulder. He can scarcely bend down far enough to ease into the front seat.

Settling in behind the wheel, I say, "Let's get that air-conditioner cranked up!" But before I can turn the key, Bob reaches over to stop me, "Wait a minute, Rita. Don't start the engine yet. Take a minute. Listen to the corn."

We roll down the windows and just sit there. Sweltering, and listening. Lost in time, between the cornstalks' shimmering overhang, a green dappled corridor as far as eye can see. Thousands of tall sturdy stalks brush against one another, whispering, rustling in the hot summer breeze. I'd heard that sound hundreds of times before, since I used to detassle corn as a kid! But I've never really *listened*.

This time I do. In the rustling, I hear Bob's voice, unspoken over the years, and silent today as well, but ever so clear. It calls to me now: *"Listen to me. See me. Understand me. Listen to my soul. This is God's Country. I find God here. God finds me here."*

How have I not heard this man before? My brother! Or seen him? Or really known him? I am humbled, sad, that it has taken me till now to meet him on this home turf. Tears well up as I reach over and touch this brother of mine. Thanks is all I manage to say. Thanks.

"Yep," he answers. "It's time to go now."

Keep Smiling

"Keep Smilin'!"

Dad always called this to us as we waved good-bye. He ended his letters to us with these words too.

Being playful and having fun was a big part of our upbringing, with our Dad being the prime Fun Instigator. The tone and spirit he set for our close-knit family is an abiding part of the Bresnahan legacy, one that, to this day, we sibs cherish and keep alive…

Moozlee-umplee-puss

My Dad loved making up pet names.

He dubbed our Mom: "Moozlee-umplee-puss."

When he proposed to her, he held out a huge fake ring from a Cracker Jack box, and asked,
> "Will you marry me, Moozlee-umplee-puss ?"

> She said yes.

Calling her this had it seasons—and its reasons. The name was magic, like "Open Sesame":

"Oh Moozlee-umplee-puss, it'll be all right."
    And it became so.

"Moozlee-umplee-puss, what do you think we should do about this?"
> And where before she had had no opinion,
> > a bright idea would arise.

Often of a waning evening, Dad would use a soft tone, and Mom would get all dreamy-eyed. They could hardly wait to get us kids tucked into bed. We were just little, and didn't know the signs.

Ours was a tiny house, and more than once, I remember hearing sweet whispers emanating from their bedroom, "Moozlee-umplee-puss oh my Moozlee-umplee-puss…"

And months later, if any of us kids ever wondered, "Where do babies come from?" you knew that, without a doubt, the answer, would have been:

"from Moozlee-umplee-puss!"

Hoo-*eeeet*, Hoo-*eeeeeee*-oo

I was born in the warm breath of my father's whistle,
   the sweetest notes ever heard.
      Hoo-*eeeet*, hoo-*eeeeeee*-oo

I came forth from those puckered lips in such lightness,
  wafting into the air like a feather,
    drifting,
      drifting
        slowly down to earth,
Dad, striding along below, hands outstretched
  ready to catch me as I swirled down to him.

I've never heard a whistle like his.

      Oh, there was a birdsong once
        a tune so close it startled me,
    but really, even a bird was no match.

All us kids were born
  from that same whistle-kiss,
and as we grew up,
  how we all waited for that Daddy sound
    at the end of each work day.

As five o'clock approached, we were poised,
  in our places near the back yard,
      waiting…
        waiting…

We could sense him coming…
    tramping over the tired railroad tracks
        up the small hill…
        down the long alley…
and then,
    right before he rounded the corner
        and came into sight,
    there it was,
        the whistle!
    Hoo-*eeeet*, hoo-*eeeeeee*-oo

The three of us would dash up the block,
    grab his legs, his hands, his pants,
        anything we could get hold of,
            all jabbering at once,
                our world now complete.

Tykes Take Mommy "Out" for Dinner...

When a Family of Six Is Too Poor to Go "Out" for Dinner
A Mother's Day Skit, 1944

Setting: *The Living Room of our home*

Director: *Dad*

Roles: *the chauffeur: Dad*
& The loving husband: Dad

> *4 Tires: Kids, ages 12, 10 (me), 6, 2,*
> *(crouching, pretending to be tires of a car, with a blanket thrown over us where fenders would be)*
>
> *The Mother: Mom, playing herself*

Props: *Two little hassocks serving as car seats rest near the two front "tires"*

Scene opens: *Dad sits in the driver's seat and "honks"*:
"Bee-beep" he says.

Mom emerges from the kitchen on cue. She's all dressed up, purse in hand.

Dad, wearing his chauffeur cap, helps Mom into the waiting "car." She sits down on one hassock, "the front seat."
    Dad closes her "car door," walks around the front tires to the driver's side, gets in and sits down on the other hassock. He turns the "key" and starts the engine.
    "Vroom, vroom."

"Tires" all shake a bit, having been coached beforehand, catching all cues from Dad's sound effects.

With a twinkle in his eye, Dad turns to Mom.
"Well, where shall we go, honey? It's Mother's Day!"
"Oh, anywhere, Farley. But what about the kids?"
"Oh they're all taken care of. Don't worry. They'll be good."

Tires giggle a little, though not on cue.

Dad pretends to drive along for a while, and then reaches back and lightly taps the left back tire three times. 2 year old Jerry's cue.

"PSsssssssssssssssssssssssssst." The "tire" flattens.

Dad gets out, and pumps up the back tire. He's fast. Tire Jerry puffs back up (with a little sib-coaching). Dad brushes off his hands, wipes them on a rag.

> *This scene repeats itself 3 more times, each "tire" in turn going flat, then "filling up" when Dad pumps for a few seconds.*

Shortly after the fourth tire is repaired, Dad "pulls over".
"Screeeeeeeeeech."

"Well, Mid, here we are at our favorite restaurant, the best in town. They're featuring a special roast beef dinner today. Mashed potatoes, gravy, and all."

"Oh goody, I love roast beef," says Mom.

Dad steps out, hurries around the front tires to her side, opens the door, and gives her a royal hand out of the car.

At that moment, all the "tires" jump up, shouting "Happy Mother's Day!" and surround our Mom with one big tire-hug.

In a jiffy, Mom changes from her dressy clothes to her apron. Proud of our performance, us kids are jabbering and laughing as we set the table and begin to cluster our crayoned home-made cards around Mom's place.

Dad heads out to the kitchen to tend his specialty: "smashed potatoes." For five minutes or so, the sound of metal clunking against metal dominates the air: it's Dad bumping the steel hand masher against the spuds pan, beat-beat-beating the potatoes and adding splashes of milk until all the lumps are out and the consistency just right.

In mere minutes, Mom calls out, "Okay, time to eat!"

The four of us scamper to our places.

Mom appears with the platter of roast beef that's been simmering in the Dutch oven since early morning. She returns for the gravy boat. And in the two-handled bowl used only for his treat, Dad carries high the mound of "ice cream" mashed potatoes.

Still grinning, we bow our heads and say grace. Dad raises his goblet, "Okay, let's clink to your Mom now!" Clinking is such a family tradition that even 2 year-old Jerry knows how to. We clink with great spirit, all around, before digging in.

MmmmmMmmmmm.

Indeed, this *is* the best restaurant in town.

Keep Smilin'

We are closing up the house we'd grown up in…
      where our Mom had lived for 60 years…
      and where Dad had died several years earlier…

We come upon a shoebox treasure
    tucked in the farthest reaches
      of her bedroom closet.

Tied with faded pink ribbon,
    it held crumbling rose petals,
and love letters between Mom and Dad,
passionate~ from their early married years…

Dad had been bumped from his railroad job…
    and if he wanted a paycheck
      in the darkest days of the Great Depression,
        he had to move by himself 100 miles away
          from Mom and his two little ones.

He'd ride the train home to us each weekend…
   and back to St. Louis again each Monday morning.
They had no phones—cell or otherwise.
We were very poor
    and letters were their only way to stay in touch.

Here's a letter from Dad
    when I was only a few months old
      and he thought my brother and I were just the cutest:

PEKIN 3/10/34

DEAR ONE –

IVE JUST A FEW MOMENTS BEFORE I LEAVE TO BOARD THE TRAIN THAT WILL TAKE ME HOME TO Y O U .. AND I HAVE ALL MY WORK CLEANED UP FOR ONCE ... AND IM JUST ALL ..ATWITTER.. WAITING TO LEAVE.. IT IS QUEER .. FROM WHAT I HEAR -- THAT I SHOULD HAVE SUCH A FEELING TO BE GOING HOME TO MY OWN WIFE .. BUT I HAVE DARLING .. AND I KNOW IT WILL NOT BE IN VAIN ONCE I OPEN THE DOOR AND HAVE YOU IN MY ARMS .. YOU – THAT LOVELY LITTLE – SWEET LITTLE -- FINE LITTLE WIFE OF ALL MY VERY OWN .. AND MOTHER OF THE TWO MOST SWELLEGANT KIDS WHO EVER CLUNG TO A MOTHERS BREAST.

I HAVENT LONG NOW TO TELL YOU NEAR WHAT I AM THINKING .. AND I KNOW YOU WILL NOT GET THIS BEFORE I WILL BE ABLE TO TELL YOU IN PERSON .. BUT HOPE YOU WILL RECEIVE IT SO THAT NOT ONE DAY WILL PASS THAT YOU WILL HAVE TO GO THRU, WITHOUT SEEING OR HEAR- ING FROM YOUR ARDENT LOVER .. AND I WILL GIVE YOU AN EXTRA KISS BEFORE I LEAVE TO REMIND YOU OF THAT ON MONDAY.   YOU HAVE HEARD OF THAT PLAY .. I LOVED HER ON MONDAY.. WELL IF I HAD ANYTHING TO DO WITH IT I WOULD NOT HAVE LEFT OUT THE OTHER SIX DAYS AND NIGHTS .. FOR EVERY ONE WILL MEAN FOR YOU THAT MY HEART AND SOUL IS ALL WRAPPED UP IN YOU AND OUR TOTS .. AND THAT EVERY MINUTE YOULL BE LOVED BY ...   *Earl.*

He was a philosopher. A scholar too,
   though he never had the chance to go to school
     beyond 8th grade, because his family was so poor.

He was a writer at heart....
When I left home at seventeen
   he wrote me long letters--
silly letters on yellow graph paper
   where he put one letter in each square...
or long skinny ones on adding machine paper
   I had to unroll as I read.

He taught me "true north"—
   the way home--
     how to find it, how to live it.
He was my lifeline
   my hero
     my bluebird of happiness.

He always always ended every letter to me, with
   "Keep smilin' honey, Love, Dad."

And... he sure kept me smilin'.
   Still does.

Spoiled

I think we were spoiled
   as kids
     by the gifts we'd been given,
        gifts we didn't even know were ours
          until many years later…
gifts unwrapped, mostly…
   not able to be wrapped.

Our family was poor,
   yet unbelievably rich
     in what our parents gave us--
       soft, constant teachings
         throughout childhood days:

> *Love comes first.*
> *Walk gently,*
>   *live simply on this earth.*
> *Remember what matters, what true riches*
> *are.*
> *Laugh a lot. Celebrate!*
> *Appreciate what you have. Be grateful.*
> *Share it.*
> *Be kind, oh be kind.*

I strive to keep their gifts alive in me…
   some 80 years later.

From the Mouths of Babes...

we listen and learn...

Children seem to possess an uncanny sense for what is needed in given situations. Their perspectives and their words continually surprise me, and remind me of what is important.

Remember How to Do Cartwheels

It is the afternoon of Jenny's Kindergarten graduation. For weeks she has been memorizing and practicing the lines of her piece. Today, when it is her turn to recite, she swishes out onto the stage, and stands carefully in the assigned spot. She opens her mouth to speak. But no sound comes. Her teacher whispers out some cues, to no avail. The blank, frightened expression on Jenny's face says it all. Putting her finger to her lips, she lowers her head and mumbles shyly, apologetically, "I…I forgot."

Jenny pauses. She shifts her feet back and forth. She looks all around, wondering what to do. A wave of embarrassed silence moves through the crowded room.

Then… suddenly her face lights up, and she shouts, "But… I remember how to do cartwheels!"

Without missing another beat, she proceeds to cartwheel clear across the stage, nearly losing her balance a time or two, before reaching the other side. Breathless, she stands tall, and curtsies, grinning broadly. Her unrehearsed feat brings wild applause, tears and laughter from the delighted and relieved audience.

More than relieved. Inspired, seems to be the deeper response.

On my way home in the car, I'm reflecting: Jenny, in all her fresh innocence, teaches me, reminds me, of some important truths: Not to define myself or measure success through any single event, or by the presence or absence of any one talent. That no matter what our age, we all have vast pools of creative resources and experience to draw from.

    I vow to keep Jenny close by.

Kindness in Disneyland:

An Angel, and Bambi

My sibs and I are hurrying along toward the theatre where a live performance of "Snow White" is scheduled for high noon. There's only about ten minutes to spare, and as always in Disneyland, especially at spring break, everyone else is scurrying too, at a frenetic pace, every which way, toward their own chosen venues. Dozens of baby strollers are being pushed along with an unmistakable urgency.

Suddenly--CRACK! A stroller or something catches my heel. Almost in slow motion, my body goes pitching forward... forward... in tiny running steps. I feel myself heading down down down-- and I crash onto the cement. I am stunned. For a moment or two I cannot budge. Everything around me stops. Every person too.

I know nothing is broken. I'm sure my total knee replacements have held. I am relieved more than anything. But breathless. And oh the pain is shooting through my leg! Security guards appear quickly and help me hobble off the busy thoroughfare onto a low stone wall several feet away. As I sit there reeling, the knot on my left knee begins bulging out before my very eyes. My hand is red too, hurting, and swelling. Two staff people from the Disneyland medical corps arrive. They ask me all kinds of questions, take down relevant information, give me some pain meds and some ice packs, and help me into a wheel chair. They assure me, "If some new or puzzling symptom arises, call us-- at any time of night or day, wherever you are, and someone will come, even to your hotel room if need be. "

My sister Mary and my brother Dick settle me comfortably at a table in one of the outdoor dining plazas. They perch my knee up on a chair next to me, find some bags of ice to put on the worst aches, and make sure I'm all right. "What if we go find something for us to eat?" They disappear to stand in line for our lunches. I stay at the table, still slightly out of it, eyes closed, reeling in pain. Icing, icing. Breathing, breathing.

All the while, at the table behind me, there's quite a commotion. A kid screaming "No! I don't want to!" An impatient Mom through clenched teeth, saying firmly, "Now you...!"

"No! Noooooo!" Naughty. Obnoxious.

Then, silence...a few moments pass, and I wonder what has taken this child's attention. Suddenly I feel a small presence at my elbow. A tiny voice asks, "What are you doing?"

I open my eyes, half-mast. A round cherubic flushed face, with delicate features and short curly brown hair, is staring into my face. The Naughty One from behind.

"Well, I hurt myself when I fell out there on the cement. These ice cubes help my knee feel better."

"Oh."

She peers intently at the icy mound, pauses, and hangs back for a moment. Then, shyly, "Want me to kiss it?"

"Why that would be wonderful!" I lift the bag of ice. She leans down and ever so gently kisses my throbbing red swelling knee.

"Why thank you! That already makes my owie feel so much better!"

I glance over my shoulder at her mother, who is tending a wee wee one. She grins at me and rolls her eyes, as if to say, "I don't know where that one came from. A minute ago she was being an utter terror." I smile back.

Little angel returns to her family, and my eyes close again.

In a minute or two, I feel the small presence at my elbow again. I peek, and this time she is carrying with her a stuffed animal. She makes this announcement: "Bambi wants to kiss it too."

Bambi is incredibly generous with kisses, sound effects and all. Kisses on my knee, up and down my whole leg, my foot, my hand, even on my neck, where another bag of ice rests.

"Ohhhhhh, that helps so much, Bambi! I have never been kissed before by a Bambi. Thank you!"

Bambi and little girl both smile, and disappear once again. A few minutes pass. Then she's back, brushing my sleeve, offering in a soft voice, "Want me to wub it a while?"

"Why yes, that would be so nice." Although the throbbing red knob on my knee cringes at the thought of being touched, I point down to my lower leg, and that's where she lays her two tiny hands. I look over my shoulder at her Mom once again for her okay. She's rolling her eyes all the more at the transformation in her troublesome daughter.

The little healing hands wub and wub and wub. Her name is Jessica, she tells me, and she is almost four years old. As we talk about Disneyland, the wubbing continues all up and down my shin, so softly, and for much longer than I imagined the staying power of a four year old to be. A light breeze, the brush of angel wings.

"Thank you, honey. You have made my leg feel so much better. You and Bambi." She grins a proud grin.

Just at that moment, Jessica's dad returns with the long-awaited lunch, and I hear happy munching sounds coming from their table. Suddenly, however, there is an ungodly shriek behind me. Then loud prolonged howling. I turn around. Sure enough, it's the sweetheart.

Her mom explains, "She was just eating her sandwich, and bit down on her own finger!"

I see Bambi lying quietly on their table. Inspiration comes. I reach over for the little stuffed animal. "Bambi wants to kiss it!" I whisper.

Bambi gambols down one arm over to the bitten finger and kisses it all around. The big tears stop, and a grateful Mom just watches, shaking her head. They all go back to eating their lunch, and leave in about ten minutes.

With a shy wave from Jessica, they disappear into the crowds.

The Microphone Tree*

I would have walked right past those little treasures; in fact I had already, numerous times. Had even crunched them underfoot, without a thought.

Today three year-old Emma notices them. Lying right there on the sidewalk, not even an inch long. She stops in her tracks, "Look, Rita, baby microphones!" She picks up one tiny stem, holds it up to her lips, and immediately begins singing into the tiny "mike." And dancing around. Right next to the busy street.

She picks up another. "Here, Rita. This one's for you!" So I start singing into it, and dancing too. Right next to the busy street.

Before we walk on around the block, she picks up several more. "One for Grandma…"

She leaves one on the top step for Molly, her favorite neighborhood dog. "Here Molly, you can bark loud now."

When we get back to the house, I remind her, "I have to leave soon, honey."

"Why?"

"To go to school, to write."

"With your writing friends?"

"Yep."

"What do they look like? Are they nice?"

"Umhmmm."

She pauses a moment before asking, "Would they like to have a baby microphone?"

"Why yes, I think they would."

So we put our coats on again, and walk the half block from her house to the magic tree. One by one, Emma tucks about 20 "mikes" into her little baggie. "Here, give these to your friends. Is this enough?"

"Yes, Emma, everyone can have one now! thank you!"

My writing friends really get into the spirit of it, and as class ends, they sing "Happy Birthday" to me, holding up and singing into their new toy.

My poem that day reads:

"We each have one.
To sing into whatever song is ours alone to sing,
our voices carrying far above
the tallest branches of the microphone tree."

* Japanese snowball, styrax

Lavender Brushing

Is it possible for a 2 ½ year old and her mommy to have a big misunderstanding?

I wouldn't have thought so until yesterday, when an unfortunate happening occurred just as I stepped through the door.

I'd forgotten my key, so Mommy (my niece) has to come let me in. She is carrying one year old Ethan, with toddler Emma hopping up and down just inches away. Emma has a metal car in her hand, and in her exuberance to see me, she flings it high up into the air.

When it drops down, it hits her Mommy's toe. She shrieks in pain, and actually starts crying.

I grab Ethan. She pulls Emma into Time Out.

"You don't throw things at Mommy!" "You don't throw things at Mommy!"

Emma doesn't know what's wrong. Just before she disappears into time out, she turns back toward me with a puzzled frightened expression on her face.

"I sorry Mommy. I sorry," I can hear her saying back in Time Out.

Now, Mommy does not realize it hadn't been intentional. After she quiets down, and has propped up her foot, applying some ice to her toe, I describe what really happened.

"You mean she didn't actually throw the car at me?"

"Not at all. Straight up."

Mommy hobbles directly in to the Time-out room to Emma. Soon the two of them emerge, tears still lingering in their eyes.

We had all intended to go for a walk, but Mommy's toe is too sore when she tries to get into a shoe. So just Emma and I venture out for a walk at Green Lake. That's a good thing.

I am pushing her in the little red car, and we're chatting with crows and seagulls, myriad doggies. We've stopped to pick up some pine cones, pretty leaves, and assorted sticks. We've been on the path only about 10-15 minutes when she looks back at me, "Need go home. Mommy. Mommy."

Now never is this energetic toddler ready to leave the lake. Never before has she initiated a return, never wanted to head toward home, even when we've been gone an hour or two. Or three. But this day it is clear that something is weighing on her little mind. She's never seen her Mommy cry. "Mommy. Mommy."

We turn around.

As we walk down the alley toward her house, we pause to pick three sprigs of lavender from a bush behind one of the neighbor's garages. Emma clutches them tightly. I begin to coach her, "When we go in the door now, give these to Mommy. They'll make her toe feel better." I am not sure she understands. Usually, after sniffing and sniffing lavender, she treats it like some kind of science project.

But this time, the very minute we step inside, Emma thrusts the bouquet of lavender at her Mommy. Who receives it gratefully, graciously. With an air of surprise.

Mommy puts her feet back up on the ottoman. Emma reaches over for two sprigs of lavender and begins lightly brushing her mommy's toe with it. (It is not even on the injured foot, but that seems not to matter at all, to anyone.) Slowly slowly, back and forth, back and forth this little girl brushes. "…make Mommy's toe feel better…"

"...make Mommy's toe feel better..."

In that moment some pent-up hard feelings seems to soften between the two of them.

All is forgiven, on both sides.

Lavender is known for its healing qualities.

    So are toddlers.

        Mommies too.

"Are You Happy?"

Just as I am about to pull out from the curb this afternoon, my niece Michelle comes running down the sidewalk, flagging me down, carrying 3 year old Emma, tear-streaked and barefoot, (knowing if she'd taken time to put shoes and sox on I would have been gone).

Puzzled, I roll down the window.

"Emma's upset because she didn't get to give you big hugs and kisses before you left."

"Well honey, I'm sorry. Just jump into the car a minute."

Emma climbs over and squeezes herself in between the steering wheel and me, straddling my legs. She holds on tighter and longer than usual.

She leans back and looks at me, "Are you happy, Ri-ta?"

"Yes, I am very happy. You make me happy, Emma. Your hugs and kisses make me happy. Thank you for coming way out here to give them to me!"

Mommy and Emma are scrambling back to the house as I drive off.

"Are you happy, Ri-ta?"

Emma asks me that nearly every time I am with her. Out of the blue seemingly--in the middle of playing cards, or munching on a taco, or walking in the park. She asks it of her Mom and Dad and Grandma too. No one knows where that question came from. It often serves as a bellwether to me though.

Less frequently, she asks, "Are you sad, Ri-ta?" or "Are you mad, Ri-ta?"

Usually that's around something specific that she's done, like sprinkling milk or water all over the counter; or knocking her little brother down.

But most of the time, it's "Are you happy, Ri-ta?"

As I drive off I am reminded of a story John Lennon told:

"When I was 5 years old, my mother always told me that happiness was the key to life. One day in school, they asked me what I wanted to be when I grew up. I wrote "happy". They told me I didn't understand the assignment. I told them they didn't understand my answer."

Namaste*

A little boy, perhaps ten years old, has just finished karate class and is strolling along Market Street in his white uniform. Walking toward the boy is a brawny man with a long ponytail, dressed simply in jeans and a T-shirt. As the two are just about to pass one another, the man steps in front of the little boy, stops, puts both his feet together and folds his hands. Then, with great reverence, he bows to the boy in the white gi, and walks on.

The boy's eyes light up, and after he takes a few more steps, he turns around to look at the man once again. Then the boy goes on his way, smiling. Not a word is exchanged, but what is communicated!

I continue on my way as well, pondering,

> *What if every child were greeted in this way?*
> *Treated with respect like this?*
> *Every adult as well.*
>
> *What kind of world would it be?*

---

* Sanskrit: "The Spirit in me recognizes, and bows to, the Spirit in you."

PREJUDICES

"preconceived opinions not based on reason or actual experience"

The following stories reveal some of the assumptions I find myself making in given situations. Though usually unconscious at first, these are judgments about people based on appearances—the way they are dressed, their age, or roles they happen to be filling at the time. Sometimes I manage to catch myself in the moment, though I'm certain that countless other assumptions slip past me undetected.

Spikes

He looked menacing. Seats on either side of him stand empty in spite of the crowded waiting area. Passengers prefer standing as they wait for the Seattle flight to begin boarding.
There is nothing extraordinary about this man. Long straggly black hair. Thin face. Fortyish. Black leather jacket. Most people would pass him by without a second glance.

Except for one thing: From inside his lower lip, on either side of his goatee: two spikes protrude—straight out. Spikes. Better than an inch long. Pointy at the ends. Yes, he looks menacing. Sinister even.

I steal several glances at him as we wait. He sits nonchalantly, alternately studying his long fingernails, his boarding pass, his cell phone. He looks neither right nor left, seemingly oblivious to stares coming his way.

Once we board the plane, there he is, in the aisle seat in front of me. There has been some mistake, clearly Delta's, and he is protesting his seat assignment being changed from business class to coach. Each time he speaks, mouth spikes dart up and down, shooting his double-edged points directly at the airline attendants.

"Unfortunately, the business class seats are already filled," they inform him, and offer all kinds of concessions. A round-trip ticket to wherever Delta flies. Coupons for drinks on the flight. etc. etc. All of which he accepts. Eventually, he settles into the flight without further protest.

I realize I have assumed certain things about this mysterious man. All because of his lip spikes:

> *He's probably a heavy drinker. Perhaps a drifter. Harsh and impersonal.*

Well, he gives the "drink coupons" away to those seated around him. I receive one.

> *Hmmmm. So, he doesn't drink.*

Five hours is a long time to study one's prejudices. A long time to shift gears. During the flight I decide to meet this man eye to eye, to speak with him. Perhaps there'll be an opportunity at the baggage claim in Seattle.

There is. While standing at the carousel waiting for the bags, I sidle up to him and ask, "Is Seattle the end of your travels?"

He looks at me, and his eyes are gentle. "No, Ma'am. I'm going up to Alaska tomorrow."

His voice is soft. Polite.

"Family up there?" I query.

Sadly: "Oh, I wish, Ma'am. No, I'm consultant for a construction project up there."

Soon his large duffel bag appears. He pulls it off, but hesitates to leave. "What does your bag look like, Ma'am?"

He waits patiently until mine comes rolling along, and when I point to it, he grabs it effortlessly and swings it in front of me with a grin. "Here you are, Ma'am."

I thank him. And we continue on our separate ways.

At this Delta carousel moment, I have scarcely noticed the lip spikes. Only this man's kind thoughtfulness, his polite ways, his smile, his soft eyes.

The Bhagavad Gita—in Iraq

I stand in a long line at Value Village waiting to buy my sister's tablecloth. Just ahead of me is a young black fellow with long dreadlocks. He is holding one large book in each hand: The *Tao Te Ching* by Lao Tzu, and *The Bhagavad Gita*. Serious, deep, spiritual writings from the 5th and 6th centuries.

I find myself surprised at his choices. He is young, in his 20's I would guess. Dressed quite unconventionally. I imagined that he'd be picking up something like trashy novels.

When he turns around for a moment, I nod toward his books. "You have excellent taste! Heavy duty reading there. I know them both. They are remarkable! Filled with inspiration!"

His face lights up. He grins. "Yeah I can't decide which one to buy. When I was serving in Iraq, my buddies kept talking about this one (the Gita)."

Whaaaat? I can scarcely hide my surprise—this is how some soldiers occupy their time!

He goes on. "You know, the entire Gita is a conversation that takes place in the middle of a battlefield."

"Hmm, I'd forgotten that."

He continues, "Are you familiar with Robert Oppenheimer?"

"Mmmmm. vaguely."

"Something he said, first turned me on to the Gita. He's a physicist who helped develop nuclear weapons. Later regretted it. When the first atomic bomb was detonated, Oppenheimer commented that it brought to mind these words from the Gita:

'Now, I am become Death, the destroyer of worlds.'"

I am speechless.

It is his turn at the register. He pays, and waves back as he departs.

"Nice talking to you."

"To you too."

Northern Lights

Our airport shuttle stops at the Westin Hotel, where a burly hulk of a man boards. His name is Lowell, and he's a "Pats" Hockey Player from Canada. Saskatchewan. Been here for his brother's wedding…He spills out all this information in the first minute.

Looking out the window, I decide not to talk, thinking: *I'm not going to be your audience, you macho, assuming we are all fascinated by every word you utter.*

Traveling along Rte. 99 in early morning offers a perfect view of the Sound, glistening…

Lowell notices this too, and begins speaking about "the beauty of Seattle…so pristine…so green…"

No one responds. Just the two of us occupy the back seat.

"It's beautiful up where I live too…the Northern Lights…they start out about this color (he pats the gray blue seat) and turns into every color you can imagine…streaking swirling, dancing across the northern sky…" He lays his head back, and closes his eyes as if looking up at a dome… "and besides, you can see every single star up there—like someone scattered tiny ice crystals all across the sky…"

      The shuttle keeps speeding along the highway in morning rush hour traffic…

The beauty of his description, his now mellow voice, tunes me back in. Slowly I turn toward him, full face, "I've heard about that. When does it happen? and how?"

"Well it's got to be very cold, below 20 degrees, very clear, and very dark. There's some pressure system…" He explains how the curve of the earth has a lot to do with it, how "the light reflects on the vapors…"

My heart has softened, opened. "You know what? The place you just described sounds so beautiful, and it makes me want to go there!"

"I hope you do."

"I hope I do too!"

Silly Silly

I am serious about silliness. I love being goofy. With my friends. With my family. And of course with children.

Sometimes my funny bone gets tickled in most unexpected places.

A Holey Time

The Harmonic Convergence. I've not thought of it for decades,
   an event observed at the same moment all over the world,
      on August 16–17, 1987,
  "a globally synchronized meditation,"
    a day "closely correlated
      to an exceptional alignment of planets."

Our meditation group agrees to fast that day in preparation. We meet at the Edmonds ferry terminal, and are transported across the waters to the little town of Kingston. From there, we drive together to Port Angeles, designated as one of the "power centers," where the spiritual energy is believed to be particularly strong. By the time we arrive, many people are already congregated, sitting in small groups on a grassy knoll. We join them.

At the appointed time, our leader invites us:
   "Let us close our eyes now in deep meditation,
     consciously joining our millions of cohorts
        around the world."
                     Thirty minutes pass. A bell rings out.

The leader calls to us:
"When you open your eyes,
   do not look around. Just…open… your eyes.
     Notice the first thing you see.
       Stay with it.
         That object will carry an important message for you
              from this meditation.
           Now…Breathe deeply…
              …and open your eyes."

Ever so softly, ever so gently,
   I do,
      ready and willing to be inspired.

My eyes immediately light upon a huge round sign blocks away,
    flashing on and off, on and off:
      Do-nuts.
            Do-nuts.
                   Do-nuts.

Transfixed, I stay glued to this sacred object.

A brief moment passes, before the leader says,
"Now close your eyes again.
    Just remain with the object you first saw.
      Breathe with it…Take it inside…
        Hear its message."
   A stifled choking pierces the silence…

I close my eyes again.

I do as instructed: I stay with "Donuts,"
   I breathe with it,
      take it inside…

Oh how I stay with it:
   "Donuts. Donuts.
     I want a donut. I want a donut.
       A chocolate one with chocolate frosting,
       and sprinkles.
    I… want… a… donut."

I've never before salivated over a mantra. Never known such a powerful one.

Afterwards, we go around the circle,
   sharing our deep insights of the day.
      Profound after Profound.

Finally it is my turn, and I have to confess…

Understanding nods scarcely hide faint smirks.

Our leader strains to glean some slight smidgeon
   of spiritual meaning from my vision.
" Well, the donut is round, like a circle. The message is:
      it's time to come 'Full circle'
         to honor 'the circle of life.'"
He stretches it even further:
   "We need to cultivate an 'emptiness' at our center,
      an openness."
Honestly? I feel he's pushing it a bit.

I listen respectfully though, not disputing his vast wisdom,
   his sound interpretive skills.

As for me though, I feel like a spiritual fraud.
   A failure.
  Because… I know that all it is, for me,
     pure and simple:
       I want a donut. *I just want a donut.*
         All chocolate. With sprinkles.

Imposter Aunt

Three young studs laugh as they tromp noisily
    down Dock D's steel ramp to the boats moored at Shilshole Bay.

Suddenly, one steps back, squints up at the walking path I'm on,
   some 30-40 feet upwards.
      and begins waving wildly my way.

I look around to see whom he might be signaling,
   but no one's behind me.
      I wish he meant me.

I wave back anyhow.

He stands another moment at the railing below.

I pause too.

He begins laughing, and shouts,
  " Oh, I'm sorry. I thought you were my Aunt Dotty.
    You look just like her!"

I catch my breath and peer down through pretend binocs, impersonating his aunt.

"Well hey, honey, it's good to see you!" I shout back. "How're you doing?"

Grinning, he takes a few steps back up the ramp. "I'm okay. How are you?"

"Good, Good. Great day for sailing!"

"Yeah it is. Hey, I gotta go. I'll call you when we get back on terra firma!"

"You will? Promise? Don't forget now!"

    We both grin, wave, and go on our way.

Strangers, joined together as long-lost Auntie
    and seafarer nephew
        for a few short moments.

Both the richer for it.

    I sure hope he calls Aunt Dotty.

Surprise Surprise

Day 1 The dreaded roofing project on our seven-story condo takes off with a BANG.
Promptly at 7 a.m. on the hottest day of the summer. Trucks roar in, motors revving.
Workers shout back and forth. Gaseous fumes permeate the air.

Incessant pounding begins. Plus scraping screeching hacking grinding and more hammerhammerhammering.
Clunksstompsthuds shake the whole building.
By the end of the day, sweltering at 97, I'm wilted, even woozy, and definitely crabby.
My head is spinning.

"How many days of this?"

To add to my misery, the staging area for the entire project is set up on the ground directly below my unit. Tar pot and all. I could spit directly down into it from my vantage point six floors up.

All the paraphernalia is there, dump trucks and the works. How did I get so lucky! The black steel crane is also positioned to perform its duties outside my deck and windows for the duration… Every load the crane hauls up must pass by my place… Down too… when fragments of the gritty flotsam and jetsam from the old roof fly wildly about. Already, dirty treasures are landing on my deck. Grrrrrrr.

Day 2 It's 7:02 a.m. I'm sipping my coffee, savoring the view out my 6th floor window:
glistening waters, gulls drifting about... Though now I have to crook my neck to see around that black steel crane. The truck below is already belching its smoke and fumes. The tar pot's bubbling. I've closed all the windows. And I'm trying to relax before heading out for the day. I must get out of here.

Then, before my very eyes, what comes drifting lazily, rakishly past my window upward to its roof destination? *A Honey-Bucket!* Just swinging and swaying in the breeze. I blink. And blink again. Am I losing it in this heat? *A Honey-Bucket?*

I laugh out loud. Oh my! May the steel cords hold. Especially when that ole Bucket comes swishing back down in a few weeks, I hope I'm not around as it sloshes past my deck with a load that's been boiling in the sun up on a tarry roof.

My laugh somehow breaks the spell that roofing project has had over me, shatters my negative spin.

Only seconds after the Bucket makes its dramatic ascent, it occurs to me: *"Resentment takes away the joy."*

These words of wisdom from Pema Chodron remind me of my joys: "Here is this gorgeous summer day, generous friends have offered me haven in their homes during the roofing; I have a play-date with little Emma today; and a walk along beautiful Shilshole with a dear friend."

"Bourgeois suffering" is what Pema would call my attitude regarding this roof project. There's Suffering. And then there's suffering, suffering I bring on myself by how I see and what I say about what's happening. Mmmhmm.

The day before, a friend had given me a Sponge Bob sun shade for my car. It reads:
"Today is the best day ever!"
"Yeah, yeah," I'd said to myself sarcastically. "With all this roofing stuff going on!"

But could it be! I do have a choice in how to meet this roofing project. I can chafe and complain, grumble and be impatient, grit my teeth for a couple of weeks until the job is over. OR I can shift my attitude. Shift my perception. I remember the old adage, "If you can't lick 'em, join 'em."

Think I'll try the latter.

Curious now, I step out on the deck to see what the container car holds when it comes down. Gravel! They're raking and shoveling the old gravel off the roof.

And guess in what form tar comes? From my perch six floors up, I see that the tar looks like a cluster of sea anemones down there. Each in a huge plastic wrap, four rows of three. Round obsidians, about the size of a kegger. Held together by heavy cardboard, from which, when cut away, two solid halves fall out.

In my observer's hat, a whole new world opens up!
                    And a strange happiness begins pouring over me…

Which isn't to say that I enjoyed the project.

And as postscript, I was not privy to the descent of the royal throne.

Rats!

A pregnant Mommy, holding her infant son, is relaxing in the living room with her mother, after a long day. Suddenly they hear a rustling and a scratching at the glass fireplace doors. Sooty from the winter's fires, the doors are too opaque to discern what is there. Except they can see two big eyes staring out at them.

"Jeff! Jeff!" they shout.
"I'm giving Emma a bath!"
They all rush to the bathroom. "There's a rat or something in the fireplace!"
"Whaaaat? A rat! I hate rats!" They've been known to gnaw on babies.
"We've got to get Animal Control out here right away. Or an exterminator."

Jeff places four urgent calls, but at late evening already, he receives no live responses. Nevertheless, at each he describes the situation, and leaves this message, "I've got a pregnant wife here; a 6 month old baby, a toddler, and a mother in law. Someone needs to come. Tonight."

They all huddle together, making new sleeping arrangements. Pregnant mom, toddler, baby, and mother-in-law head downstairs. They must not sleep upstairs, if at all.

Jeff, alone with the mystery intruder, begins shoving the living room furniture away from the fireplace, filling in spaces he fears the rat might run to or through. Around 9:30 p.m. he is relieved to receive the call, "Someone will be at your house by 11:30."

Sure enough, that's when the doorbell rings. There stands a big burly guy holding a huge cage, rigged so that nothing can get around it. "I'm Andy. Let's see what you got."

Jeff watches at a distance as the exterminator places his cage at just the right angle around the fireplace for instant capture. Then, ever so slowly and gingerly, Andy opens the glass doors.

> No creature rushes out. Stunned, it just blinks and blinks its eyes.
> "Quack Quack!" Keeps blinking, as if to say, "What took you so long?"

Andy swoops up the duck, tucks it under one arm, and strolls over to the front door. He opens it with one hand, and with the other, releases his capture. The dazed duck waddles unsteadily off into the late night air.

"That'll be $100."

Jeff hurriedly writes out the check, not in the least begrudging Andy the money.
"It's worth every penny," he declares.

> Now, in the next few days, if you spot a young mallard near Green Lake covered with black soot and ashes, you'll know: he's the one.
> He has the inside scoop.

Quirky

It is early on a cold snowy morning.
I am driving along Aurora Avenue to my downtown office,
   hearing the radio announcer drone on
      about all the school closures that day…
         one after another.

"And Immaculate Conception is running two hours late."

My quirky brain leaps at these words, twists them all about.

   The Immaculate Conception running two hours late!
      Sacrilegious images begin swirling in my mind
         mixing eerily with snowflakes on the windshield.

            I have to pull off to one of the side streets…

I imagine the Virgin Mary, at the appointed time and place,
   lying on a soft white mat, in missionary position,
      in great readiness and anticipation, awaiting the sacred moment…

Hearing the stunning news on the radio, Mary sits up abruptly, "What the…?"
   She wraps her blue cloak modestly about her,
      and begins wringing her hands.
         "It's running late?? Two hours! What ever shall we do?"

These words she addresses to the Angel Gabriel hovering close by, who's been summoned to witness this momentous occasion. Gabriel simply shrugs…

At this point the holy scene begins to fade…

I regain my composure…enough to resume driving.

So… I'm sorry to report…
    I don't know if, after being delayed a couple of hours,
        the Immaculate Conception ever got back on track,
          if it ever *did* happen…
            or if the Church Fathers only *claim* it did,
              or--if the poor Lady still lies, patiently waiting…

Really, I have no idea.

        I just hope the kids got to school on time that day.

Weighing In

It is supposed to be just an ordinary lay-over on the way to our family reunion.
My sister's flight from Eugene and mine from Seattle arrive on schedule in Los Angeles, where Mary and I meet so we could travel the second leg of our trip together. Not having seen one another for months, we have lots to catch up on, and we find ourselves laughing out loud, having a good time with one another.

About forty-five minutes before our flight is scheduled to take off, a ticket agent steps over to the two of us saying in a near-whisper: "We may have to ask two passengers to stay behind when this flight leaves, but we won't know until a minute or two before departure time. *If* that becomes necessary, would you two be willing to wait for the next flight in about 2 1/2 hours? We'd give you each $600 and meal vouchers."

Mary and I look at each other grinning. Hmmmm. $600. Each! Only 2 1/2 hours later? "Sure!"
"Good. We'll let you know, but be ready either way."

Of course the two of us begin conjecturing why *we* were chosen, and no one else.
Mary's take: "Well I think it's because they noticed how good-natured we are, and happy. You know, we've been laughing so hard, and having fun together."
My spin: "They figure we can handle a long wait, and have a good time doing it."

We feel pretty smug.

"Hey, while we're waiting, let's talk about what we could do with our $600's!"

· 53 ·

"Let's go to Greece!"
"Oh I've always wanted to go to Turkey!"
"Why not do both?!" Thus we launch our plan.

About ten minutes before scheduled departure, all the other passengers board the plane to St. George. Meanwhile, Mary and I huddle together, waiting, wondering if United has forgotten about us. Finally, the agent steps over. "We do definitely need your seats."

"Oh great! Are you overbooked?"

"No, it's not that. You see, the ground crew has just finished weighing the final *cargo* to be loaded. They've informed us that, as we suspected might be the case, with the two of you on board, the plane would *exceed* its gross tonnage. It'd then be over the maximum weight limit.

The Bresnahan girls weigh too much for the Friendly Skies? "Gross tonnage"?!

It takes us a while to regain our composure. And salve our wounded pride. We'd *love* to know the *actu*al conversation that took place behind that desk, how they must've looked the two of us up and down.

Actually though, the humiliation is short-lived, a small price to pay. Because you know what? We've just booked October flights to Greece and Turkey.

Failing My Physical

Following are the results of my latest complete physical, one conducted by four year old Emma. Using the doctor kit she received for Christmas, she performs the examination:

—Listens to my heart with her stethoscope (slightly askew): "Now cough!" I do. ("Mmhmm. That's good.");

—Takes my blood pressure. Wraps band around my arm and pump pumps. Checks the reading: ("2-4-6. That's good");

—Gives me a shot (pokes too hard);

—Applies bandage on my finger (it sags limply);

—Lastly she examines my ears, using her Princess flashlight and the proper plastic instrument. First one ear, then the other. She runs her fingers all around every inch of the lobes.

Finally, dropping the flashlight, she declares with an air of great authority:
    "Well, your ears… are too big."

She pauses, before adding,
    "But they're clean. They're very clean."

With that, the "doctor" abruptly leaves the room. Our appointment is over, just like that. No recommendations. No chance to ask any questions. No explanations. Nothing.

I look around. Grave doubts begin to arise regarding this physician's credibility, her professionalism. She has left her instruments strewn all over the floor!

She might actually be a quack.

Regarding my ears?
I am seeking a second opinion.

We Are Crones

"Crone" is a word that existed tens of thousands of years ago when women's life patterns were conceptualized in three stages—Maiden, Mother, and Crone. Although the word has been used derogatorily for decades, we now use it intentionally "to reclaim the respect and admiration given in times past to old women for their courage, endurance, and wisdom… So we come together in circles and gatherings to support each other."

These next stories offer a window into the lives and values of some of today's crones who are in their 70's and 80's and 90's. We bring into the open aging issues we wrestle with, and stances we choose to take. We realize how life can change in an instant. These stories reveal how challenges in old age might be met, and a new life envisioned. We survive. We stand strong.

We are Crones.

Yellow Blanket Babies

In times gone by, when a new baby arrived,
  visitors could stop by outside the hospital nursery
    and peer in the windows
      at the tiny beauties inside.

Blue blankets marked the baby boys,
  Pink, the baby girls.

  Oooohs and ahhhhs.

I remember pressing my nose against the window,
  proudly pointing, "She's my baby sister!"
    I was eleven for Mary.
And thirteen when Patti arrived.
As oldest girl, I was junior mom
  to all my younger sibs!
    So, I knew a lot about babies.

But this I did not know,
  until at Crones Counsel,
    a woman in her 70's
      walks up to the stage,
        and tells us:

"There were babies under yellow blankets too.
    Not in the same room as the other babies.
      Hidden away."

She catches her breath before continuing:
"I was one of those yellow blanket babies…

In a back room, behind a door marked DNS/DNP:
>Do not show.
>>Do not publish.
There was no window at our nursery.
Nothing was wrong with us,
>except our moms couldn't keep us."

She pauses. "Many of us were later adopted and loved. But there was always a question in our minds about why we were given up…
>Now, my hunch is that there may be several yellow-blanket babies in this room. If you were one, hidden away those first precious days of your life, I invite you to come up on the stage and stand with me, proud, in the fullness of this light."

Silence…..Tears…..
>No one moves. No one speaks.

Then, in the hush…
>from the back of the hall, one woman stands…

>>Slowly she makes her way to the stage.

Then another… and another…
>until there are six.
Six women who'd been wrapped in yellow.

Hugs and tears on the stage.

We in the audience stand… as one body…
>in tears too, silently honoring, bearing witness.

A woman in the front row begins singing,
"Oh, you must have been a beautiful baby…"
>and we all join in…
"You must have been a wonderful child…

You must've been a beautiful baby
'Cause Baby, look at you now!"

    We sing it through again, lustily.

Those of us in the front rows begin surging forward
       to the foot of the stage.
Looking up, we begin pointing…
"Oh, look at that one. Isn't she cute!"

"I want that one."
      "That one!"
           "Oh, that one! You're adorable!"

The yellow-blanket women step off the stage
      into circles of tears mingling with theirs,
         into cradling arms…

Turd into Trillium

The Madrona woods are alive with awakening spring. Two dear Crone friends stroll along the lush paths, 87-year-old Eileen holding tightly onto the arm of her 60-year-old friend, Judith, whose eyes must see for them both. In the past five years or so, Eileen's macular degeneration has left her nearly blind, with scarcely the capacity even to discern shapes. This is particularly tough for a former professor, an author and avid reader, a life-long walker. Young friends like Judith ease her losses somewhat, and make it possible for her to still enjoy many of these pleasures.

Being outside together is a delight for these two friends. Today as they walk along drinking in pine and blossom fragrances, and listening to sweet birdsong of spring, every so often they pause a moment at a sight Judith knows Eileen too would appreciate but is unable to see. Judith begins describing in detail:

"Here are the red-flowering currants, Eileen. Their small fuchsia flowers are peeking out from the lobed leaves…And oh, the skunk cabbages are just starting to pop up."

They stop at the salmonberry, Indian Plum, and other surprises. At each treasure Eileen draws close, sometimes reaches out towards it, nods enthusiastically, seeing only in her mind's eye the scene Judith has just painted. Many of the plants are easy for her to visualize since she remembers them from spring in the woods at her beach place and even from her childhood.

After a while, the two emerge into a clearing where the sun is beaming down. Suddenly Eileen stops abruptly, leans down, and shouts, "Look! A Trillium!" The sighting of this three-petaled white flower above a whorl of three leaves is a rare sight in the Northwest, and thrills anyone who's lucky enough to spot it.

However, to Eileen's exclamations of delight, Judith says nothing.

"Look! Don't you see it!? A trillium! A trillium!" Eileen is pleased that even through blurred vision, she can still discern a beloved flower.

Judith tries to control herself. She can scarcely speak. When she finally regains her composure somewhat, she manages to sputter:

"Eileen. Oh Eileen. I hate to tell you, but what you're looking at is **not** a trillium. It's …it's a turd! You're pointing at a dog turd!"

"Whaaaaaaaat?!!"

"Yes, I'm sorry to say, it is not a trillium, but… it's… a dog… **turd**."

Sure enough, they're in damp green forest trillium habitat, and the white blob down there does have an amoeba-like faint trillia shape. Eileen leans down as far as her cane allows, peering closely, and would've been tempted to caress a trillium, but resists, taking Judith's word for it. Instead, she nudges the blob slightly with her cane, the resistance a confirmation all its own. The two double over in laughter.

"How'd a dog do *that*?" they wonder, finally concluding, "This turd has been here a loooong time. Turned white from baking in the sun, don't you think?"

The two friends go giggling on their merry way.

I've often wondered what kind of person I'd turn into if I lost my vision, and my ability to walk, or to walk freely--two capacities I count on, and treasure the most. How would I continue? Would I want to? Could I be gentle with my own increasing limitations? Would I allow my vulnerabilities to be, and to be seen? Could I be like Eileen?

I hope so.

A Breath Away

I want to tell you a story, but in order to tell it, I first must share two earlier events that inspired, primed and planted the seeds for the final story. The events happened on three successive days, as part of Crones Counsel, an annual nation-wide gathering of crones. In September 2008, the Counsel was held in Seattle, at the Doubletree Hotel, the setting for the following events.

On the Counsel's opening day, Mahtowin, Dakota Native American elder, shares the following narrative. In her own words:

There is a place known to most of us now as Mount Rushmore. To natives of the plains, it is the heart of Turtle Island (North America). It is said that if you were to fly over the Black Hills, you would see that the hills have the shape of the human heart. This place was the last stronghold of the native people, and they fought desperately to save it from invasion.

In the early 1970s a group of about one hundred Native Americans decided to visit the top of Mount Rushmore to hold a healing ceremony for the mountain that had been carved and gouged into the faces of former presidents. On the assigned morning of the ceremony, we gathered at the bottom of the mountain and began our ascent to the top. As the group walked, we sang, chanted and prayed. After several hours, we arrived at the top and formed the ancient sacred hoop of the nation. Young men made up the outer circle with the older men forming the second circle. The third circle was comprised of the young women and in the center were the grandmothers and children. This has always been the way of the sacred circle. The core of the nation rests with the grandmothers and the children. Without these two, a nation is believed not be able to continue.

Once we had established our place within the circle and had begun our ceremony we were startled by the sudden arrival of a group of National Guards- men. The soldier in charge went immediately to the elder men who were leading the ceremony and told them we had to disperse immediately. Words went back and forth among the soldiers and the elders, and tempers began to flare and voices were raised. An order was issued and the young soldiers encircled us with their shouldered guns. The young men on the outer circle shoved the soldiers back and chaos began to reign. Another order was issued and the young soldiers unharnessed their rifles from their shoulders and pointed them into the circle. More natives began to push the outer limits of the circle and most there knew that soon one or more of us would be shot. In the span of a few moments we were standing as enemies did 100 years ago.

Just as shots were surely to be fired, without a word spoken between them, the grandmothers rose to their feet in unison. Each grandmother took the hand of a child near her and began to walk to the outer rim of the circle. Those who had been pushing and shouting at the soldiers moved and made a space for each pair as they fanned out to the edges of the circle. It would not do to knock a grandmother or child to the ground, so, out of respect, space was made for them. As the grandmother nearest to me came face to face with the young frightened soldier in her path, she reached out her hand and said, "Grandson, will you walk your grandmother down the mountain?" Each of the other grandmothers had said something similar to the soldier in her path and the top of the mountain was embraced in *absolute silence. The soldiers hung their rifles on their shoulders again and offered their arms to the grandmothers to assist them down the mountain. As I looked at the young soldier in front of me, I noticed that he had tears rolling down his cheeks.*

Without a word spoken between them, these wise old women defused a very dangerous situation and probably saved several lives that day. They needed no weapons of war to create a peaceful solution. Their power came from a place of love and a deep and ancient wisdom that is known to all women.

Used with permission of Mahtowin

Mahtowin's words were very powerful and stayed with all of us during a workshop entitled "Code Purple" offered on the second day. The workshop focused on crones using our power to affect social situations, political or personal, "acting up to call attention to something they feel needs exposure to the light." It was billed as a time to brainstorm ways that crones can make a difference, ways for us to speak up, or learn to defuse a conflict situation. Animated discussions revolved around concerns, resources, strategies, and other possibilities.

"What brought you to this workshop?" the facilitator asked each participant. My response: "I want to learn to be intuitive like the grandmothers on the hilltop…so in tune with what is happening that I know inside myself, without words, what is called for in a given situation. And then, have the courage to act from that knowing."

Now I knew when I spoke that such an intangible learning was far beyond the scope of this ninety-minute workshop. But I had to say it. I do believe that intention is powerful. For me, it's opening myself up to be guided. Especially when stated aloud, it takes on a life all its own, and often holds an important teaching. My experience also tells me that somewhere within intention lies the wisdom one seeks. And the courage.

The next day an opportunity arose that called for courage and action.

❦

It's the third and final day of Crones Counsel, and many of us are talking over lunch in the restaurant near the lobby. Earlier in the day, another group had arrived in the hotel—a "Psychic Faire" according to their banners. Palm readers, Tarot experts, and astrologists have been setting up, and some have already begun their "readings."

Shrill shouting suddenly rings out in the lobby "Repent or Perish!" "Your work is evil!" "Jesus can save you!"
Glancing over, we see four burly men and one woman carrying menacing placards. Each wears a black T-shirt with pointy blood-red-orange hellish flames licking at words across their chests: "Repent or Perish." Bearing bibles, the five are advancing on the room of psychic practitioners, screaming their message: "Jesus can save you!"

A lone slender woman from the Psychic Faire is attempting to dissuade those spewing fire-and-brimstone, "Please be quiet, and stop disturbing us."

"Jesus Saves from Hell!" "Know Your Bible!" "What you do is evil!" Angry voices reverberate off near-by walls as the group attempts *to force its way into the Psychic Faire.*

At this point a hotel manager appears on the scene. Softly and politely, he addresses the taunters: "Please leave. This is private property...

Please leave, you have no right to intimidate our guests. I don't want to have to call the police."

The protesters pay no heed.

One crone closest to the commotion steps toward the group. Though nearly blind, she sees clearly what needs to be done. She quotes some peaceful Bible passages (using a bit of poetic license). "Shake the dust off your sandals and go on your way." "Why do you throw your pearls before swine?" They disregard her too, and the clamor continues, louder than ever.

Almost as one body, other crones, this writer included, rise spontaneously from our tables of twos and threes, and make our way over to stand with our sister crone and the manager. The crones say nothing, simply link arms, gradually forming a solid phalanx of grandmothers four or five across, four rows deep. We place ourselves less than a foot away from the protestors, thus blocking their access to the Psychic Faire.

One crone whispers, "Let's quietly walk them out."

In total silence the crones begin slowly edging themselves forward. Simultaneously, the intruders find themselves inching backward in response. Eyes neutral, the crones look steadily into the accusing, angry faces. The grandmothers link arms with the manager as he repeats, "Please leave. This is private property. You need to leave now."

Five minutes? Ten minutes? The time is immeasurable as grandmothers have inched their way nearly fifteen feet along the side hallway, simultaneously and peacefully backing the taunters toward the side exit. Suddenly, when only a couple of feet from the doors, the bully in front, his face in the manager's, shouts: " "Don't touch me! Don't get in my face, you are too close...don't shove me!"

"Sir, I am not pushing you. It is the women behind who are pushing *me*."

This shouter stops in his tracks. He looks up. Crones are only a foot away from his face, but it's as if he sees our grey heads, our wrinkled and calm faces for the first time. Surprised, he stands disoriented, disarmed, as if nothing prepared him for this.

The other protesters keep shouting in our faces.

We stay a breath away. However, each time the most vociferous of the angry crew pauses, the crone closest to him whispers in his ear, "Jesus didn't scream like this." Like a mosquito she pesters him time and time and time again, "Jesus didn't scream." "Jesus never raised his voice."

We shuffle.

We pause.

We breathe. A human wall of grandmothers, we inch forward again. Forward. The taunters, back. Back.

Almost without realizing it, the harassers find that they have stepped backwards, so far backwards, that their backs are now touching the heavy metal exit doors. A hotel employee arrives from the outside, and opens the doors. Slowly the grandmothers usher the angry and somewhat-bewildered protesters out through the open doors into the parking lot. In disbelief, and slightly subdued, still they scream their epithets. "You've been warned!" they tell us, "Don't say you haven't!"

The doors close on their voices and their menace.

Inside, we heave a deep collective breath, then simply return to our tables and unfinished lunches. No words can express what we have just experienced, though instinctively we realize this has been a sacred moment.

> *Surely Native American grandmothers from the mountaintop have been with us in spirit, and linked arms on this day.*

Just Build Fires Together

We're the earliest guests to arrive at the hostel this evening. Three crones, exploring the area around the Pacific Rim, hiking along this wild and rugged southwest coast of Vancouver Island. At the end of our 3rd day out, our camping plans dampened by a persistent rain, we've decided to check into the Surf's Inn in Ucluelet BC. After we unpack a bit and settle into the second floor dorm, we head downstairs to lounge awhile in the spacious living room. Soon the place begins to bustle with Australians, Germans, Brazilians, indeed a whole cosmopolitan mix from around the world. We can detect the accents, though everyone is speaking English.

The three of us are enjoying a glass of wine together in the parlor, when a very young German couple strolls in, arms around each other, he, trying to help his sweetie get warm. Catching sight of the huge fireplace, Hans (we decide to call him) says, "I'll just build a blazing fire here for you," promising her she'll be toasty in no time.

Our Romeo selects the perfect logs from the towering stack of firewood, places a few together, and scrounges up a bit of kindling. He finds some matches, and proceeds to light one, after another, after another in his futile attempt to get a fire going. That he has little experience in this fire business is apparent. The logs look lovely, but they are so close together, there's no room for them to breathe.

Meanwhile, across the room we seasoned Crone campers are biting our tongues, quietly observing the unfolding scenario. Finally, seeing the frustration building on Hans' face, Susan calls over to him, "I think we have some paper in the car that would help get the fire started."

"You do?"

"Yeah. Would you like me to go out and get it?"

The German seems surprised. "In the rain?"

"Sure." Susan trudges down the long slippery steps, across the muddy parking lot, and fetches the 4-day-old Seattle Times, tucking it under her raincoat to keep it dry. She hurries back in, shakes off the wetness, and delivers the paper to Hans. Grateful, he begins laying thick chunks of it on top of the logs. Flat.

Now what to do? Susan is appalled. And speechless. It is a delicate situation. A couple of old ladies don't want to embarrass this dashing young buck, especially in front of his darling.

Molly can stand the tension no longer. She leaves her comfortable perch on the couch, crosses over to the fireplace, and kneels down beside Hans. Susan does too. Ever so gently, Molly coaches, "You know, what I've found is that if you take only a bit of paper and twist it like this, it helps a lot." She places her demonstration under the logs. Hans follows suit. When 6 or 8 scrunchies are poking out from under and between the logs, Susan says, "Let's move the logs apart a little so that there's some air between them."

That done, the three fire-builders breathe a collective sigh, and sit back on their haunches. "Now are we ready?" asks Hans.

"Now," echo Molly and Susan. "And let's light it from underneath."

With new-found confidence, Hans sets a match to their masterpiece. Susan and Molly blow hopeful breaths ever so lightly, and the flames leap upward.

The two sweethearts cuddle back under their blanket, close to the fire as possible, soon lost in their own world. Hans' lady is gazing at him adoringly, marveling at his fiery genius. "Oh Hans, this is wonderful!" she gushes. "I'm not cold anymore!" As reward, she plants quite a kiss on his cheek, her eyes sparkling. His too.

A minute or two later, Hans, grinning, glances across the room at us, and with a big wink, remarks, "You know, this is what Germans and Americans need to do. The whole world really. Get together and build fires. Just build fires together, like we did tonight. And sit in front of it. What kind of world would that be?"

We all continue on with our evening.

As I'm drifting off to sleep that night, this young man's words keep echoing, echoing in my mind. Simple words, yet provocative, even profound.

Yes, Hans, we'd welcome that kind of world.

Good Medicine

With tears welling up,
   Ellen, age 70, softly places in my hand,
     a tiny crocheted heart.

Its threads stretch back years,
        years we've been walking this walk together.

            She'd been driving along that easy summer day…
              CRASH
                The car that killed her sister sitting next to her,
                mangled her own arm…
                  "Oh, my spinning arm!
                        Will I ever spin again?"

Such pain. Deep deep grieving.

Long hours, months of rehab, rehab, rehab
    especially on those spinning muscles,
       nerves, torn crushed…
          all feeling of touch, gone…
her spinning fingers like two empty spaces
    rubbing against one another.

"I must spin again
   I must spin again…
      My life depends on it."

And it did. That much was clear.

An idea comes to Ellen.

She begins saving cotton balls
　one by one
　　　from all her medicine bottles.
　　　　　until she has handfuls....
　　　　　　　then bagfuls.

She has plans for these balls.
Her swollen fingers tingle with anticipation.

Slowly, ever so slowly...
　　　　　spinning muscles begin returning,

With the first painful joyous moments
　　　back at her beloved wheel,
　　　　　she begins spinning cotton balls into thread.
Wincing at times, she spins on and on,
　　　creating spool after spool
　　　　　of pristine thread.

Painstakingly
　　from this "medicine bottle" thread,
　　　　she crochets tiny soft hearts
　　　　　　to give away...

With tears welling up,
　　she places one gently in my hand.

I want to live like that:
To gather the losses of my life,
the crashes...
bitter medicine in fragile bottles...
Then spin them into soft tender thread,
weave that thread into love,
to give away again.

Beginnings and Endings

We welcome new beginnings
and
we are continually faced with small
endings and losses

as well as life and death ones.

Love Cycles

Yesterday she did it!
Suddenly we noticed she'd disappeared,
and we couldn't find her in the usual places…
    and there she was, sitting on the potty!
She'd pulled down both pair of pants by herself,
for the first time, and there she sat as if it were the most natural
thing in the world.

        "Why are you all surprised?"
She leaned down to get a good look at the magic yellow stream.
"My pee is yellow!"
And we were all marveling. Clap clapping.
"Big Girl!" "Emma Emma!"
We put one Dora sticker on the wall
    and another on the back of her hand.
And she was oh so proud! Grinning and dancing twirling.
      The rest of us dancing dancing too.

Our family loves to celebrate such marker events, and Emma will experience many over the coming years. There'll be the whole school cycle; and at eleven or twelve when she begins her monthly cycle; and cycles of young love…
      Children grow up, so fast. No denying that.

…When it's time, I want to talk to her about the cycle of life—not the birds and the bees part—
    but about how we are born, and how we die. Everyone.

I'll tell her about those long winter weeks when she was only two. I started each day with quiet hours sitting in Intensive Care, breathing, just breathing with my closest friend Lynn, as she lay dying. Afterwards--every single morning--I'd drive straight over to play with Emma. Seeing me, she'd jump up and down, shouting "Weela Weela!" hugging my legs, grounding me back on this earth. Great joy, and great sorrow, weaving themselves together at once. Parallel universes. Yet touching one another. In both, a cycle of life, and of love, being lived to its fullest, its deepest.

In kind of slow motion at first, I'd find myself moving from the timeless zone of Intensive Care… to be swept suddenly into the magical world of chasing an ornery toddler around the house. How rich, how privileged I felt, to experience the whole span of life in a matter of twenty minutes, a few miles. How profound: to move from the quiet ending of one precious life to rolling around in the beginning of a precious new little life.

A time to be born, a time to die…

Those wintry days I began discovering how much it is all one, with so little difference between those worlds. I stand in awe, stepping back back back to honor this Mystery weaving through our lives. The same radiance, the same spirit danced in my friend Lynn's eyes as in Emma's.
It is all one: the great mystery in which we all dwell, the mystery of how life begins, of how life comes to an end.
Each is so precious in its own way.
Each so beautiful. So wonder-ful.
Each holds the eternal living and the eternal dying in each moment.
Each brings a keen awareness of what matters in the end.
    And in the beginning.
        And all the in betweens.

Two things matter most, it seems:

> The first: Love. Give love, see with eyes of love, everywhere.
> Be kind, oh be kind. Touch tenderly. Stay connected. Care.
> Just care.
> And…

The second: Be with, simply be with, no agendas.
Stay aware, ride the waves of what is happening, moment by moment.

> With a dying friend. With a rambunctious toddler.
> Just be there. Enter in. Follow where, and how, one moment opens, leads to the next.

That's what we are called to do.

Such is the cycle of life I want Emma to know. I'll tell her too how the part she played during many sad, demanding months, buoyed me up, made all the difference. I'll share the piece I wrote about the time she wanted a Dora Band-Aid the same place on her arm as she watched her mommy put on mine. How she was learning that human beings gather around a person who's hurting. How they are kind and do what they can to help them feel better. And that she gets her turn too. Everyone does.

Yes, little Emma was, and is, like a Band-Aid for me whether she knows it or not. She does protect me, helps with the healing. She hurts in the same places I do, helps me cry, helps close tender wounds.

And like the Dora Band-Aid, Emma even makes the hurts look a bit cheery, makes me smile in the midst of them. Helps me remember what's under the Band-Aid,
> what's under the scab,
>> and deep under the scar.

Reminds me how love cycles through our lives.
Helps me know:
the scar tissue is worth all the love
—and even—
worth all the hurting too.

Born Again Boots

My battered hiking boots have had a good life. They've forged their way through many a back country. They've kicked the dust up craggy mountain peaks, rugged, steep and strenuous. With great care they have navigated sub-alpine meadows and fragile tundra. These steel-toed giants have cushioned aching feet from teetering rocks; they have fjorded rushing mountain streams.

Sometime in my 60's these boots begin to notice: "Hey, Rita is limping more and more. We only get to hike short distances."

"Yeah. She's got serious knee problems."

One surgery follows another and another and then another.

The Boots? They occupy front row seats in the living room closet. Petulant complaints rumble out from the crack under the door: "Hey, let us out! This is terrible! Sacrilegious! To simply be stuck in here. Don't you remember we've trekked hundreds of miles, even up sixteen Colorado peaks over 14,000 feet?! We can't stand this just sitting around. We deserve better!" They are outraged, restless…

…Gradually though, the voices fade…

For over a decade, their soles remain ever-hopeful whenever the closet door opens. "Today, Rita, today?" they ask eagerly, refusing to believe they've been benched, and are gradually being retired.

Never are they chosen. Not even picked up as a possibility. Patted with reassuring hands every so often, but always passed over. One awful day they are placed in a plastic bag and shoved toward the rear of the closet. Crushed.

As the years go by, the disappointment becomes discouragement, which turns into despair, especially on weekends, when other boots are trekking happily off to breath-taking adventures…They begin to resign themselves to a long dark closet life of staying home, inactive and invisible and unappreciated…

Until one winter day. That was when the owner of these boots, this writer, took a terrible fall. No. Not even in the mountains, but in my own front yard. I could scarcely pick myself up from the offending sidewalk crack, even with the help of my friend Phil who happened to be right there. Phil managed to half-drag me into the house, settling me into my cushy recliner. He fetched dusty crutches from their hideaway, then rounded up a supply of ice, juices and snacks. He had to leave then, after assuring me, "Call me if you need anything…"

The hours pass by… Do I lose consciousness? I'm not sure. I just know my body is aching all over, especially my right ankle. In spite of TLC and long icings, it begins swelling and purpling and screaming. After a miserable endless night, my neighbor Shelly drives me to the nearby health clinic. X-rays reveal "an avulsion fracture in the lower tibia." The doctor prescribes icing, rest, elevation, pain pills.

"Besides," she cautions, "that ankle needs to be protected, and it needs extra support. I suggest you purchase an air cast—or…" Pausing, tentative, she eyes this grey-haired out-of-shape woman as if already knowing the answer… "…do you by any chance have a pair of sturdy hiking boots? With high tops?"

My heart leaps. My eyes close softly. Something long forgotten begins stirring in me... a mountain spirit, transporting me to the greenest valleys, a fragrance of virgin forests. Stunning vistas, where lofty snow-capped summits rise in every direction...

❦

Suddenly I become aware of a strange uncomfortable silence. Oh, I'm in the doctor's office! The doctor is waiting, expecting an answer. I open my eyes and grin. "Oh, yes! I have a wonderful pair of hiking boots!"

The doctor's eyebrows lift in surprise. "Good. Boots are even better than a cast."

I can't wait to get back home. With an air of excitement and anticipation, I dash—er, hobble-- into the house, and throw open the closet door.
"You're on!" I declare, reaching down for my long-neglected treasures.

"Us? Today? Us?" Their red nylon laces quiver in disbelief. Then excitement. "We're going up to the mountains?"

"Well, to the mountains, Kids, but not ones you've traveled before. Rough and rugged terrain of a different kind..."

There are mountains and there are Mountains... I explain the situation at hand.

"Whatever!" they shout in unison. Not in a resigned or disgusted "whaaat-everrrrr" but in a grand eagerness to be redeemed, to be of service, to be involved in any way possible. "Whatever! Thank you oh thank you!"

With affection for these faithful friends, I scrape the encrusted mud from their well-worn soles. As I shake them against one another out on the deck, sweet mountain dust flies in all directions. We stand ready for our new adventure.

I pull on my born-agains nearly every day now. Converted to in-town boots especially in the rain, they take me to the store nearby. Out for short walks. They render me brave enough to maneuver my way around the Mariners stadium for a game. Up and down precarious Key Arena for a WNBA "Seattle Storm" nail-biter. They tackle the steep stairways of elegant 5th Avenue Theatre, where, surefooted, and otherwise dressed in my finest, I am able to enjoy an opening night show.

That my hiking boots have been resurrected has changed my life. Not only do they support my healing ankle, but they lift my spirits. They've made a believer out of me…
I too feel born again! Alleluia! I walk differently inside these boots: no longer so tentative, no longer feeling so vulnerable. Rather, confident and strong. Taller. More alive.

These ole hiking boots have had a good life. That they're all scuffed up, shrunken a bit, with seams fraying and treads wearing thin doesn't seem to matter. Knowing that wherever they step is holy ground, they just keep on hitting the trail, smelling the wildflowers, one foot in front of the other. That's all that is asked of them.

    Of me too.

Our Tears Run Together

"Oh, tell me, what was it like?" she gushes.

How would I tell, that as a young seventeen year old I had to sever every emotional tie. Every feeling. Every aspect of personal history. In order to be worthy...

How would I tell that eighteen years later, how I'd longed for someone to make me laugh, remind me not to take things so seriously, draw me out from my isolation. Someone to go with me to buy real clothes, someone to shelter and protect me during those naked first weeks and months "out"... Someone to reassure me, tell me I was stronger than I thought I was. Someone to help me piece back together all of the Rita that had been so carefully dismantled over those years.

>*Sent back out floating into empty space...*

>*Like a ghost walking an earthly landscape.*
>*A misfit.*

>*No rehab provided. No half-way house.*

"Oh, tell me, what was it like?"

"Well, it was like going through a nasty divorce."
    And that's all I'd want to say about it.

Still the inquisitive persist. "Why'd you leave the convent, after 18 years?!"

>*Do I tell that the young woman's body rebelled first*
>>*then her sensitive mind*
>>>*her spirit--*
>>>>*all broken.*
>>>>>*It was not pretty.*

She dared not believe…
    that shackles of eighteen years
      could ever fall away
   shackles of an innocent teen's promise,
      of outdated dogma
    of unbearable guilt if she tried to break free.

How describe the darkest night-- ushered out the side door in disgrace?
  How convey futile attempts to wipe the sense of shame—
     and the despair of failure
       off her cheeks…

That history of mine, regretfully, is often the only piece of information a new acquaintance knows about me, or chooses to remember. At first meeting, questions have been fired at me in rapid succession, with great curiosity.

"Why'd you go? and why'd you stay? Eighteen years a nun? So why'd you leave?"

Usually I repeat: "Well, leaving was like going through a divorce. And that's all I have to say about it."

They persist. "Well, I mean, what was it *like?*"

It's not easy to explain. Sometimes I simply suggest reading Karen Armstrong's convent experiences in her book "Spiral Staircase." I was "in" three times longer than she.

Early on, challenging responses were thrown at me when someone first learned that piece of my history. Rarely in the 70's was it received favorably. Often it sparked an angry tirade about that person's mistreatment at the hands of nuns. Always unsettling for me, I struggled with how to process it all, how to protect myself from feeling personally attacked, how to reconcile the not-always-the perfect nun memories in myself that would get triggered. And if it were my choice, I'd not share that part of my history for a long while. Otherwise, I found myself stuck into a pigeon-hole:

Who I am= former nun. That fact, that identity trumped everything else, every other accomplishment, every other role…
And there have been many over the years.

Quite long ago, an unexpected path to reconciliation and healing presented itself: a weekend's Native American Healing Circle in Oregon, led by a Cree elder from Canada.

On the first morning, Eddie the Cree Elder, opens the Circle with his own story, and for an hour he recounts the abuse he suffered in his boyhood—being placed in boarding schools, a common practice at the time. He describes continued prejudiced treatment against him and the other Indian kids—at the hands of…yes, the nuns. Abuse by the nuns—physical and emotional, intellectual too—and especially spiritual.
You must embrace the Catholic faith. It is the only way.
Wipe the Native Spirit out of your bones. No Great Spirit!

The Elder weeps as he speaks. For how many long decades has he wept?
How many times, told this story? And still he weeps.

His pain, his words pierce me to the core. I can scarcely breathe, scarcely remain in the circle. The air closes in around me. I want to run. Run! Run!
Somehow I have taken on myself the guilt of the nuns who had abused him. All through a sleepless night I wrestle with it … How to resolve such relentless collective guilt?

In the light of early dawn, I realize what I must do.

The next morning, Eddie opens the circle, holding high the talking stick.
"Who would like this now? I know there are those who must speak."

Some Spirit-Greater-Than-Rita nudges my body over to stand in front of him. Red-faced and choking, I divulge… haltingly… my own nun-history.

Then I find myself kneeling before him. Reaching out both my hands, I plead,
    "Eddie, in the name of those nuns who mistreated you,
        I beg your forgiveness.
        We have harmed you, and we are so sorry.
        Can you find it in your heart to forgive us?"

Tears begin streaming down his face. Mine too.

I can scarcely bear the ancient pain in his eyes.

        A great silence. He cannot not speak.
        All is hushed in the room.

I can look at him no longer. I bow my head.

His hands, quivering, lightly touch.

I lift my eyes. He is nodding, slowly nodding. Twice his chin touches his chest, each time resting there momentarily. Standing tall in his full dignity, his gaze extends up up beyond my face, into the skies.

He reaches into his shirt for a red Cree kerchief and pats his eyes…
    Brushes my face with it too, saying, "Our tears run together."

Taking both my hands, he lifts me to my feet.

Boat Whisperers

Strolling along the marina one morning, I was feeling kind of down and heavy, though I didn't know exactly why. Even though I was passing by the same boats as always, their names began leaping into my consciousness in a different way, at a different level. I started saying the names aloud, nodding to each as I passed, for an instant stepping into the moods their names express. Arriba! Celebration Allegro Vivace Brava!

This lifted my spirits.

I paused a moment at the railing and began to ponder. Each name represents a tiny window into the life of its owner when first he/she laid claim to that boat. How visionary seafarers must be, using metaphor to proclaim their identity, their path at the moment, their connection to a loved one or to the world about them: how they see it, how they see themselves, how they want to be seen.

All phases of a human being's life are reflected in this softly rocking marina collage. "Quixote" and "Derring-Do" rub prows with "Final Approach," who faintly remembers those "Siren Song" days of yore. And of course, "Invictus!" swears there'll never be a "Last Tango" for this sailor.

That morning, I realized that the story of our life cycle, from beginning to end, was being whispered to me by the names of boats docked at Shilshole Marina. Starting at the beginning of life:

Chrysalis
Halcyon Days
Imagine
Dream Catcher

Different Drummer
Siren Song
Wanderlust
Solo
Sea Trek
Sojourner
Carpe Diem
Full Speed
Discovery

Glass Slipper
Priority
Delight
True Love
At Last
Side by Side
Prime Time

Indian Summer
Life Is Good
Serenity
Moon Light
Reflections
Evening Run
Weary of Gold
For Sale

Last Tango
    Lone Star
       Eclipse
          Delirium

    The Ultimate
      Final Approach
    Nirvana
  Paradise
Shalom

Whose names are these? Whose voices? Whose call? Whose life?
Whose journey?
What path followed?
    From whence do we come?
        toward what destination do we move?
            Following true north—or not?

> *From cruising yacht to humble dinghy,*
> *we share this vast sea together,*
> *whether safely anchored in port*
> *or tossed on stormy waters...*
> *Poets, seafarers, philosophers, all...*
> *from "Chrysalis"*
> *to "Final Approach"...*
> *each ultimately*
> *answers the call*
> *to lower our sails...*
> *to come to rest...*

...All this, from a morning stroll...
    which brings me to this question:
As a window into my life at this moment...What would I name my boat today?

    What would you name yours?

Footprints

Footsteps
   leave footprints.

I look behind
   noting where others have trod…
      whose steps I have followed,
         at times breathless…

 My sturdy leather boots
   have scuffed their way
      up one scenic trail after another
         fragrance of tall cedars filling the air
            ecstasy echoing back and forth against canyon walls
along banks of iris,
   hillsides of purple lupine and scarlet paintbrush,
      dotted with golden yellows,
         saucy wildflowers tucked into tiny crevices
            where nothing should grow.

Boots tread lightly on fragile tundra
   to the very summits…
      vistas unimagined
         and wild winds too.

Chill and warmth take turns coursing through my bones.

Deep into the valley these feet have trod as well
   mired there,
      unable to catch their breath
         or discern a way out of darkness
            lost…
or, even if they knew the way,
     too exhausted to ascend
         to the end point, the starting point.

        Today,
I look back, remembering, and grateful,
   to those who have traveled the path before me
     whose footsteps I have followed…
        Today,
    at this late season of my life,
as my hiking days fade to fewer, shorter, and less intense,
      at this crossroads I ask:

What footprints do I leave along the trail now
   What cairns build, to point a way that's smoother,
     not fraught with sudden drop-offs…
   How to clear underbrush, tangled vines,
       exposed roots
     for vague shapes
        appearing in the distance?

Jubilee Reflection

Climbing
  climbing
    a ladder into the spacious sky
      through rolling mists
        and billowing clouds…

In this, my glorious 80th summer,
    I pause at the uppermost rungs…
  to gaze fondly down
    upon this gracious earth
      upon these generous days
        upon the children… oh, the children…
      and upon all my beloveds,
        who have held me, stood by me…
      all my days.

    My heart is full to overflowing…

I climb the sunsets one by one
  more slowly now,
    more deliberately,
      ascending the ladder that,
        some distant day, or near…
        I will step from…
          fall from…
            fly from…
              into…
            the Great Nowhere
              …into…
            the Great Everywhere…

I am not afraid…

    of falling…

        or of flying…

            or of the Spacious Sky…

About the Author

A Seattle psychologist, social worker, and educator, Rita Bresnahan has been a "professional listener" for more than six decades. Her writing reflects the meaning, and often the poetry, she finds in everyday kinds of happenings—through her favored themes of insight and transformation, children, and humor.

Rita is author of the book *Walking One Another Home: Moments of Grace and Possibility in the Midst of Alzheimer's*. Her stories and reflections have appeared in *Chicken Soup for the Woman's Soul* and in *A Time to Weep, A Time to Sing: Faith Journeys of Women Scholars of Religion*.

Rita can be reached at *namaste7@comcast.net*

For more about the author, see the Ballard Writers Collective website:

www.ballardwriters.org/2013/01/13/rita

~ "Rita's stories enter your mind the way she enters a room—on a wave of love and energy, full of life."

~ "Rita's writing is playful, wise, earthy—often penetrating."

~ "Rita invites us to our laughter and our tears. She blesses us by sharing her own."

~ "Rita's stories are so human. She relates with deep heart and soul."

~ "Rita writes with a stream of consciousness through love and connection."

~ "The love with which Rita sees and portrays friends and family, from her time with a two year old to her last goodbye to a friend, rises from the page to mingle with your heart."

~Cancer Lifeline Writing Buddies